MARTIAL ARTS for Kids

# A LOOK AT
# WRESTLING

Cara Krenn

Lerner Publications ◆ Minneapolis

Copyright © 2025 by Lerner Publishing Group, Inc.

All rights reserved. International copyright secured. No part of this book may be reproduced, stored in a retrieval system, or transmitted in any form or by any means—electronic, mechanical, photocopying, recording, or otherwise—without the prior written permission of Lerner Publishing Group, Inc., except for the inclusion of brief quotations in an acknowledged review.

Lerner Publications Company
An imprint of Lerner Publishing Group, Inc.
241 First Avenue North
Minneapolis, MN 55401 USA

For reading levels and more information, look up this title at www.lernerbooks.com.

Main body text set in Mikado.
Typeface provided by HVD.

**Editor:** Annie Zheng **Designer:** Mary Ross

**Library of Congress Cataloging-in-Publication Data**

Names: Krenn, Cara, author.
Title: A look at wrestling / Cara Krenn.
Description: Minneapolis : Lerner Publications, 2025. | Series: Lerner sports rookie. Martial arts for kids | Includes bibliographical references and index. | Audience: Ages 5–8 | Audience: Grades K–1 | Summary: "Wrestlers pin, hold, and throw down their opponents to win a match! From wrestling basics to styles to competition, young readers will love learning more about this popular sport"— Provided by publisher.
Identifiers: LCCN 2024012895 (print) | LCCN 2024012896 (ebook) | ISBN 9798765647998 (library binding) | ISBN 9798765662106 (paperback) | ISBN 9798765656310 (epub)
Subjects: LCSH: Wrestling—Juvenile literature.
Classification: LCC GV1195.3 .K74 2025 (print) | LCC GV1195.3 (ebook) | DDC 796.812—dc23/eng/20240321

LC record available at https://lccn.loc.gov/2024012895
LC ebook record available at https://lccn.loc.gov/2024012896

Manufactured in the United States of America
1-1011024-53360-7/18/2024

# Table of Contents

| Chapter 1 | What Is Wrestling? | 4 |
| Chapter 2 | Wrestling Basics | 8 |
| Chapter 3 | What to Expect | 14 |
| Chapter 4 | Wrestling Champ | 20 |

| Glossary | 24 |
| Learn More | 24 |
| Index | 24 |

CHAPTER 1

# What Is Wrestling?

Wrestling is one of the oldest sports in the world. It is also a martial art.

In wrestling, two people try to force each other to the ground. They can do this through holds, throws, and pins.

## CHAPTER 2
# Wrestling Basics

Wrestlers wear special shoes and a tight uniform called a singlet. Some wrestlers also wear ear guards and kneepads.

There are many kinds of wrestling. Greco-Roman wrestlers only use their arms and upper bodies against opponents. Freestyle wrestlers can also use their legs.

## FUN FACT

**Greco-Roman and freestyle wrestling are both Olympic events.**

Wrestling is done on a mat. Wrestlers earn points for throws and holds. Matches end when a wrestler pins an opponent's shoulders to the ground.

## FUN FACT

A wrestling match is called a bout.

CHAPTER 3

# What to Expect

Wrestlers learn moves during lessons. They learn how to grapple, or how to grab someone else.

Wrestlers also learn how to escape from holds. During a hold, a wrestler keeps another wrestler from moving.

Having a strong lower body is important. Wrestlers can practice lunges and squats to build their strength.

# UP CLOSE!
## Wrestling Stance

**Stand with your feet apart. Put one foot out in front. Bend your knees. Hold your hands in front of you, and keep your elbows bent. Make sure to look forward.**

CHAPTER 4

# Wrestling Champ

Wrestlers can compete in tournaments. They wrestle people of similar size.

**FUN FACT**

Some wrestlers go on to become pros.

Anybody can have fun with wrestling! Are you ready to try?

## Glossary

**martial art:** self-defense skills that people practice for sport

**opponent:** someone you compete against

**pin:** to hold an opponent's shoulders to the ground

**throw:** a move where a wrestler lifts an opponent and tosses them to the ground

## Learn More

Downs, Kieran. *Wrestling*. Minneapolis: Bellwether Media, 2024.

Krenn, Cara. *A Look at Judo*. Minneapolis: Lerner Publications, 2025.

Ridge, Yolanda. *Wrestling*. New York: Lightbox Learning, 2024.

## Index

freestyle wrestling, 10–11

grapple, 14

Greco-Roman wrestling, 10–11

holds, 6, 12, 16

singlet, 8

## Photo Acknowledgments

AleksandarGeorgiev/Getty Images, p. 5; JoeSAPhotos/Shutterstock, p. 7; Bob Daemmrich/Alamy, p. 9; Tim Nwachukwu/Getty Images, p. 11; Kayla Wolf/NCAA Photos via Getty Images, p. 13; Jim West/Alamy, p. 15; GTS Productions/Shutterstock, p. 17; Lintao Zhang/Getty Images, p. 18; Ahturner/Shutterstock, p. 19; Ni Minzhe/CHINASPORTS/VCG via Getty Images, p. 21; Naomi Baker/Getty Image, p. 23. Design elements: str33tcat/Getty Images; ulimi/Getty Images; Tuomas A. Lehtinen/Getty Images.
Cover: Al Powers/Zuffa LLC/Zuffa LLC via Getty Images.